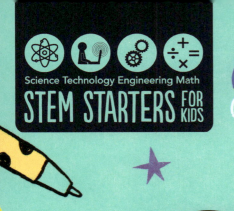

ZOOLOGY ACTIVITY Book

Written by Sam Hutchinson
Illustrated by Vicky Barker

FOR YOUNG READERS

Text and illustrations copyright © 2025 by b small publishing ltd.

First Racehorse for Young Readers Edition 2025.

All rights reserved. No part of this book may be reproduced in any manner without the express written consent of the publisher, except in the case of brief excepts in critical reviews or articles. All inquiries should be addressed to Racehorse for Young Readers, 307 West 36th Street, 11th Floor, New York, NY 10018.

Racehorse for Young Readers books may be purchased in bulk at special discounts for sales promotions, corporate gifts, fund-raising or education purposes. Special editions can also be created to specifications. For details, contact the Special Sales Department at Skyhorse Publishing, 307 West 36th Street, 11th Floor, New York, NY 10018 or info@skyhorsepublishing.com.

Racehorse for Young Readers™ is a pending trademark of Skyhorse Publishing, Inc.®, a Delaware corporation.

Visit our website at www.skyhorsepublishing.com.

Please follow our publisher Tony Lyons on Instagram @tonylyonsisuncertain

10 9 8 7 6 5 4 3 2 1

Design and art direction by Vicky Barker
Additional cover illustrations by Ste Johnson

Manufactured in China, September 2024
This product conforms to CPSIA 2008

ISBN 978-1-63158-731-3

WHAT IS ZOOLOGY?

Zoology is the area of science that studies animals. It is a branch of biology. Scientists who specialize in zoology are called zoologists. They investigate what animals look like, how they behave and where they live.

WHAT IS STEM?

STEM stands for "science, technology, engineering and mathematics." These four areas are closely linked, and zoology uses skills from all four of them. If we understand how animals live, we can help protect them and maybe even learn from them.

Science   Technology   Engineering   Math

SO MANY ANIMALS!

There are millions of different species of animals in the world. Some of them are up to 100 feet in length, others are the size of a pumpkin seed. Some can run at 43 miles per hour (mph), while others walk at around 0.3 miles per hour (mph). The saying "stranger than fiction" means that the truth is often weirder than anything you can make up. This is definitely the case with the animal kingdom!

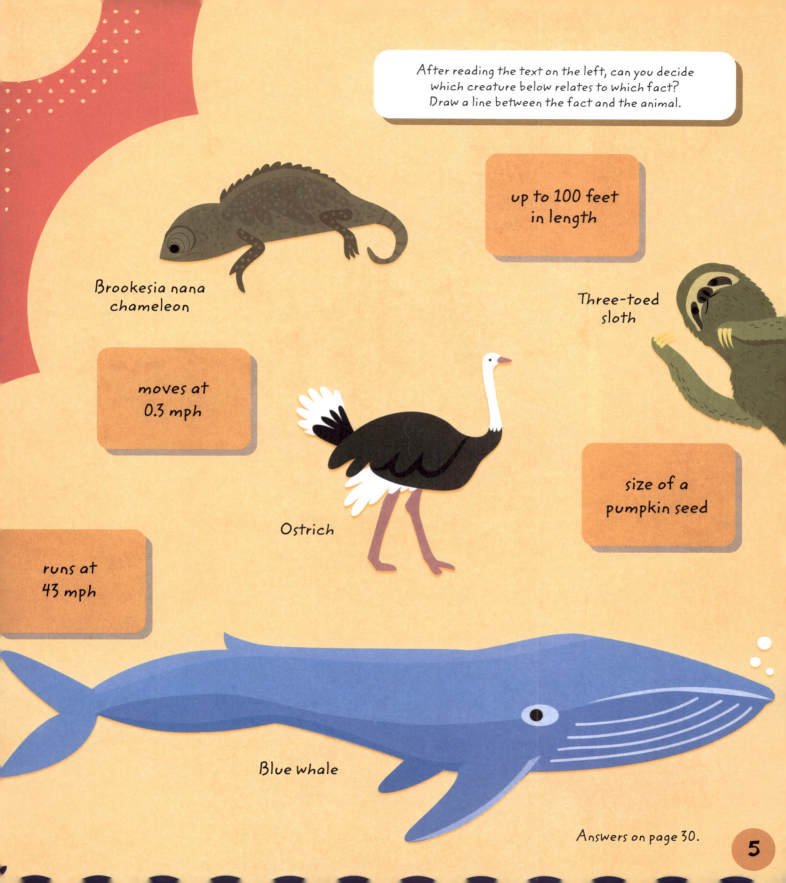

NO BONES ABOUT IT

Zoologists sort animals into different groups based on their features. This is called classification, and the first step is to check if the creature has a backbone. If it does, it's called a vertebrate. If it doesn't, then it's called an invertebrate. The animals within each group can still be very different from each other but they all have that one feature in common.

Classify the animals on these pages as vertebrates or invertebrates. Check your answers on page 30.

Dragonfly

Vertebrates!

Invertebrates!

Only 3% of all animals on Earth have a backbone!

The remaining 97% are invertebrates.

CREATING DIVISIONS

When classifying vertebrates and invertebrates into smaller groups, zoologists study how an animal's body grows and how it has babies. Even if two animals are very different, they can still be in the same group.

Vertebrates are a really diverse bunch! Read what makes these animal pairs similar. Then write under each one what makes them different. Check your answers on page 30.

Adélie penguin

BIRDS
- lay eggs
- have feathers

Golden eagle

_____
_____
_____
_____

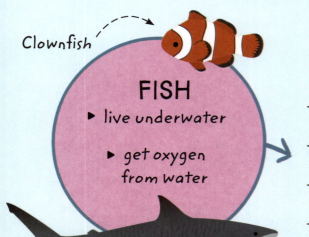

Clownfish

FISH
- live underwater
- get oxygen from water

Tiger shark

_____
_____
_____
_____

8

NATURAL HABITATS

All animals need food, water, and shelter to live. Animals adapt to live in their natural habitat, which means they develop certain features that help them to survive there.

Desert

Polar

Fresh water

Forest

Grassland

Mountain

Can you find these habitat words in this word search?
Words can read backwards, forwards, up, down and diagonally.

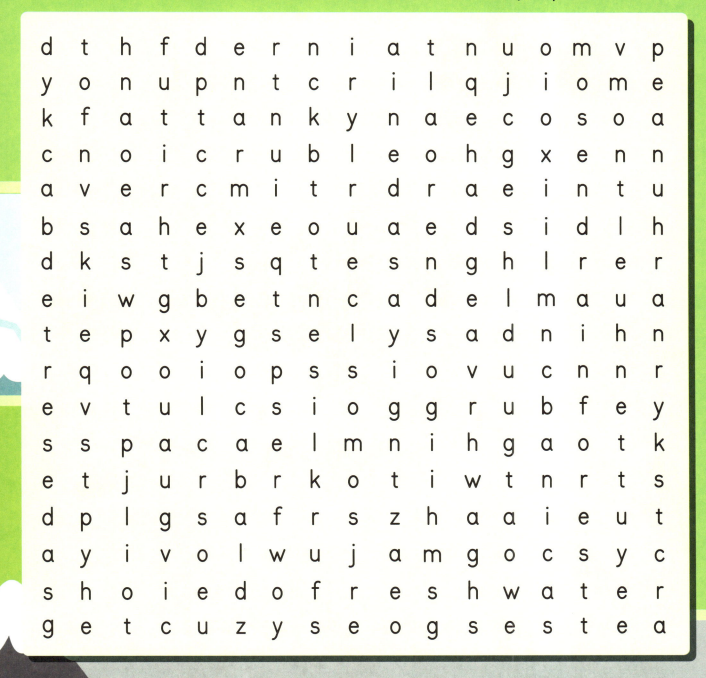

Grassland   Mountain   Ocean
Polar   Forest   Rainforest
Desert   Fresh water

Answers on page 31.

GROWING UP

Birds and most reptiles lay hard-shelled eggs, from which their young will hatch. Most mammals give birth to live young that need milk to grow. Most fish and amphibians lay soft eggs in water, which go through quite big changes before becoming adults.

Discover more about how animals go from baby to adult with this quiz. Check your answers on page 31.

1. All baby animals need milk from their mother to grow.

    ◯ TRUE?   ◯ FALSE?

2. Birds aren't the only animals that lay eggs.

    ◯ TRUE?   ◯ FALSE?

3. Blue whale babies are 37 feet long when they are born—about the length of a bus!

    ◯ TRUE?   ◯ FALSE?

4. Sometimes the male animal carries the babies instead of the female.

    ◯ TRUE?   ◯ FALSE?

5. Frogs are the only animal with four stages in their life cycle (frogspawn → tadpole → froglet → frog).

    ◯ TRUE?   ◯ FALSE?

6. Polar bears give birth to just one cub.

    ◯ TRUE?   ◯ FALSE?

13

ADAPT AND CHANGE

Adaptation is when a type of animal gradually changes over time. The Arctic fox has slightly shorter ears and a shorter muzzle than the red fox. It also has fur on the pads of its feet. These are adaptations that help it to keep warm. One other important adaptation is that its fur changes color, from white in the snowy winter to brown in the summer when the snow and ice melt away.

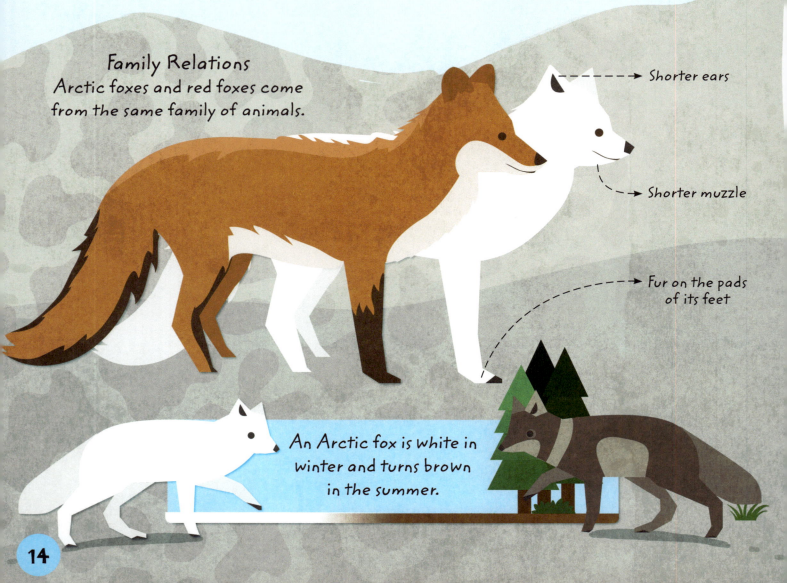

Family Relations
Arctic foxes and red foxes come from the same family of animals.

Shorter ears

Shorter muzzle

Fur on the pads of its feet

An Arctic fox is white in winter and turns brown in the summer.

Think about your home town.
What sort of adaptations would be helpful for you to have?
Draw the new you!

THEY HIDE IT WELL

One way that animals adapt and survive is camouflage. Having a certain color of fur, like the Arctic fox, is a sort of camouflage. But there are many examples of much more elaborate camouflage in the animal kingdom.

Jaguars and leopards have darker spots in their fur, which help them stay hidden as they stalk their prey. When zebras stick together in a big group, their black and white stripes make it hard for lions to see them separately.

Below is the start of camouflage patterns that certain animals have. Can you complete them and identify which is which? Answers on page 31.

DAY AND NIGHT

Another example of smart adaptation is developing certain senses, such as seeing or hearing. Nocturnal animals are good at finding their way at night. Foxes and wolves can see well in the dark, and bats use echolocation, which is where the echo from their squeak helps them understand what's around them.

The opposite of nocturnal is diurnal! Diurnal animals are most active during the day.

GLOW IN THE DARK

While some creatures are good at seeing in the dark, others are good at being seen in the dark. They have certain chemicals in their bodies that cause them to give off light. This amazing phenomenon is called bioluminescence. It's an adaptation that helps creatures attract a mate or, in some cases, startle any predators. The anglerfish dangles some bioluminescent flesh in front of its face to attract other fish, which it then eats!

Most bioluminescent creatures exist in the ocean, but on land you might spot a firefly, beetle, or even a glowing mushroom.

Glow-worms

Headlamp beetle

Jellyfish

Deep-sea sharks

Fireflies

TOO MANY!

Energy from the Sun feeds all of the animals on our planet. But they don't actually eat the sunshine! Plants need this energy to grow, then some animals eat the plants and other animals eat those animals. In this way, the Sun's energy travels through what's called the food chain.

Zoologists study food chains, and when lots of food chains overlap it's called a food web. Food webs can easily become unbalanced if one of the animals grows or shrinks in number.

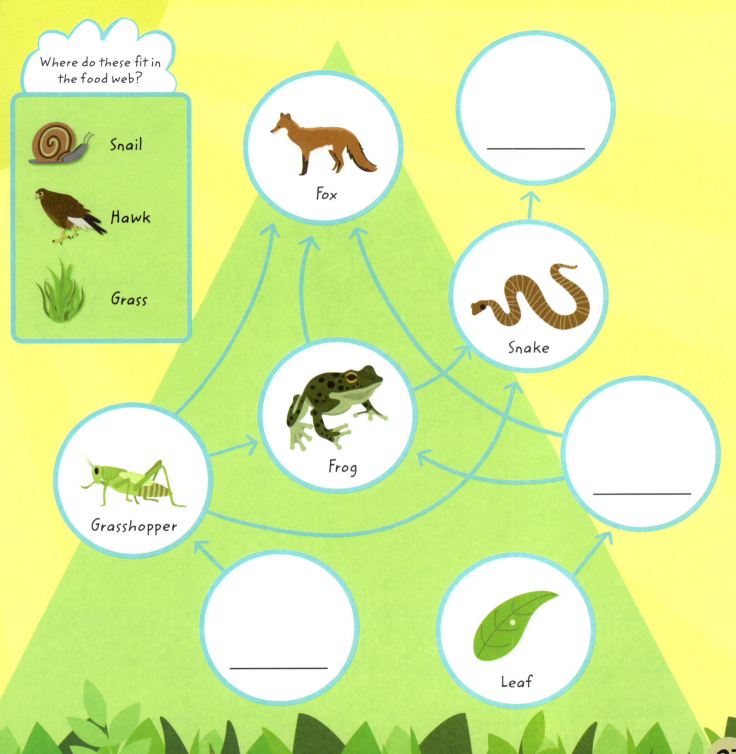

DON'T COUNT THEM OUT

One really important job for a zoologist is to track endangered species, or animals that are struggling to survive in their natural habitats. It might be that they haven't adapted quickly enough for any changes in their habitat or, more likely, their habitat has been damaged by human activity.

When zoologists study endangered species, they can learn more about what is happening to them and how we can help them to survive.

HIT THE ROAD

Some animals move long distances around the planet. This is called migration, and animals do it for different reasons. Wildebeest travel just under 1900 miles in a year to find the greenest grass.

Grey whales swim all the way down the coast of North America, from their feeding grounds in Alaska at the top to Mexico at the bottom, where they have their babies. That's around 5,000 miles—one way!

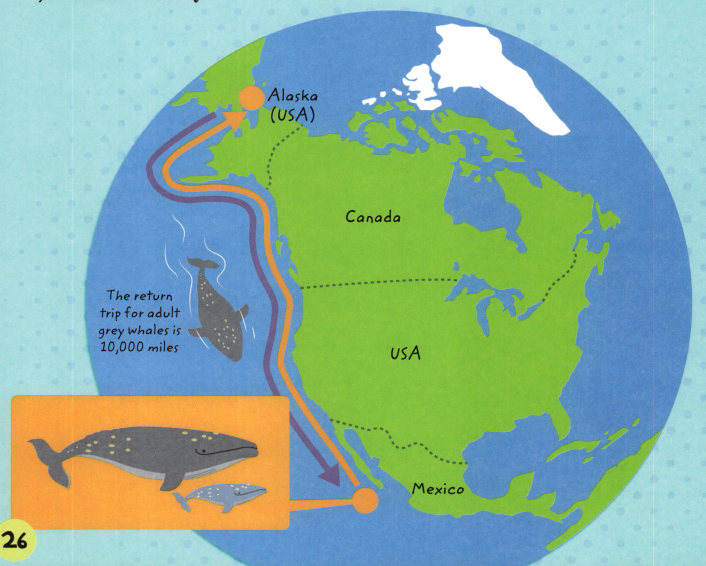

The return trip for adult grey whales is 10,000 miles

Crack the code to reveal the name of the animal that travels the longest distance when migrating—over 24,000 miles, one way! Check your answer on page 32.

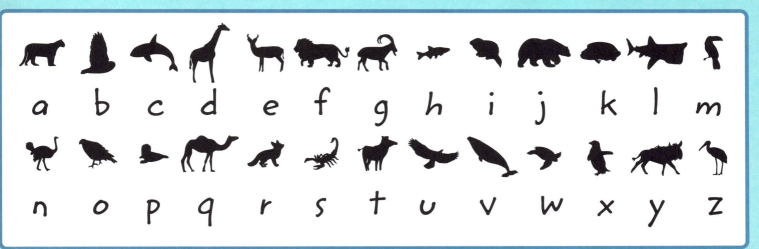

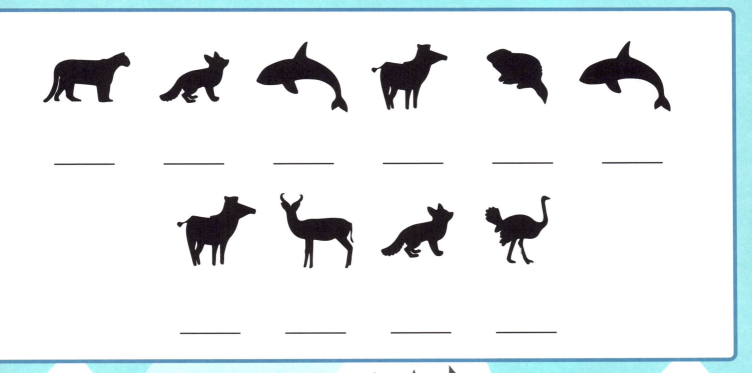

MAKE YOURSELF AT HOME

It's not just wild animals that capture a zoologist's attention. Zoology includes studying domesticated animals, such as pet cats or dogs. A domesticated animal's natural habitat is to be with the human that looks after it—it would struggle to survive in the wild.

Most domesticated animals are useful to humans for a particular reason.

What do you think these animals can be used for?
Match the animal with the task!

Riding or pulling heavy loads

Hunting vermin

For meat, milk, skin, and wool

For meat and eggs

Protection and help with hunting

Answers on page 32.

29

ANSWERS

pages 4-5

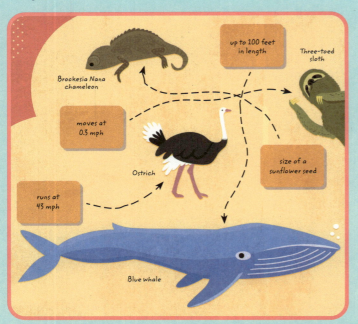

- Brookesia Nana chameleon — size of a sunflower seed
- moves at 0.3 mph — Three-toed sloth
- Ostrich — runs at 43 mph
- Blue whale — up to 100 feet in length

pages 6-7

Vertebrates	Invertebrates
Dolphin	Butterfly
Frog	Jellyfish
Hawk	Crustacean
Giraffe	Dragonfly
Snake	
Arctic fox	
Fish	

pages 8-9

BIRDS
- Penguins cannot fly but they can swim.
- Eagles can fly and they have very sharp talons.

MAMMALS
- Wildebeest eat grass, have horns and run around on land.
- Seals eat fish, don't have legs and can swim underwater.

FISH
- Tiger sharks can grow to over 13 feet.
- Clownfish grow up to 7 inches.

REPTILES
- Boa constrictors don't have any legs!
- Crocodiles have legs.

AMPHIBIANS
- Frogs can jump long distances.
- Newts have tails.

Here are some differences but you might have thought of more!

pages 10-11

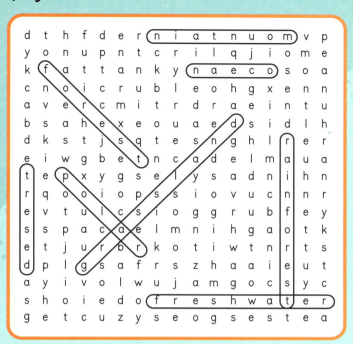

pages 12-13

1. FALSE—only mammals (such as cats or elephants) need milk.

2. TRUE—reptiles, insects and even some mammals (platypus!) lay eggs

3. FALSE—they are ONLY 23 feet long, which is about half a bus. Still - that's a big baby!

4. TRUE—male seahorses and sea dragons carry the babies!

5. FALSE—most amphibians (such as frogs) and insects have four stages.

6. FALSE—it can be one cub, or even three or four, but it's usually two.

pages 16-17

Giraffe

Zebra

Tiger

Cheetah

Snow leopard

pages 18-19

pages 22-23

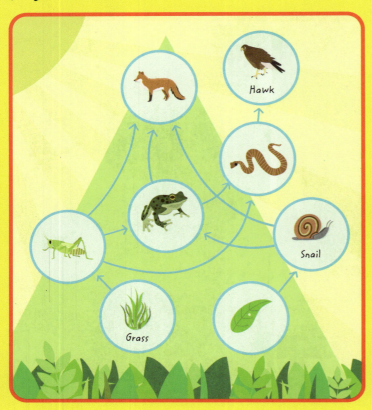

pages 24-25

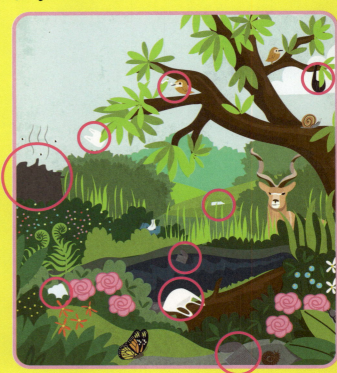

pages 26-27

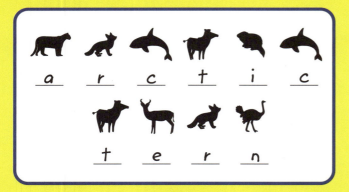

How did you do?

pages 28-29

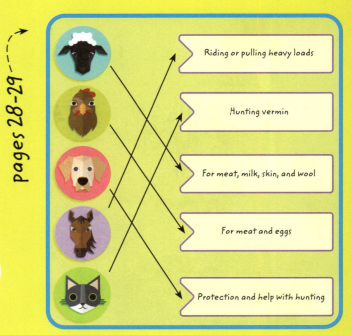